BREAD OF HEAVEN

REFLECTIONS OF THE WORD

BILLY EVANS

Written By Sharron Hardwick

DEDICATION

IN LOVING MEMORY OF BILLY AND CERI EVANS

DEDICATION

This book is written by Sharron Hardwick for the Evans family in loving memory of Willam (Billy) Evans and his beloved son, Ceri Evans.

ACKNOWLEDGMENTS

NEW LIFE CHRISTIAN FELLOWSHIP PEMBROKESHIRE
WWW.NEWLIFECHURCHPEMBS.COM

BILLY SHARING THE WORD: LOVE - CHAPTER 6

BILLY IS PHOTOGRAPHED HERE AT NEW LIFE CHRISTIAN FELLOWSHIP
WITH HIS BELOVED WIFE, RHONWEN EVANS

CONTENTS

Acknowledgments

1 CHANDELIER

It doesn't matter how fancy a chandelier is, without electricity it just doesn't work! You'll be left in the dark if it's not connected to the power source. A flick of a switch is all it takes, if all the connections are right.

So how do we get the power?

A Dr, Luke, wrote a book we call Acts. He reports on events just after Jesus' death on the cross and his coming back to life, the resurrection.

We read that Jesus asked his followers to wait in Jerusalem.

These people had experienced a life with Jesus, seen his power, witnessed his death and saw him alive again. To top it all, they then saw Jesus taken into heaven, and all they had was these memories and the instructions to wait.

But they weren't just hanging around like a disconnected chandelier, they acted while they waited. They prayed together, and were all in agreement with one another.

These faithful followers were not to be left alone. They trusted Jesus' promise that the Holy Spirit would come to them, filling them with the power to fuel real faith and action.

Sometimes we are left waiting. We wonder what's going on. We can worry, doubt and grow fearful, or we can try to trust, as these followers did.

They soon saw the promise fulfilled. Luke reported that they were all in one place, unified in faith, then SUDDENLY there was a rush of wind, a mighty power and what looked like flames upon the believers. They spoke in every language and onlookers were amazed, some thought they were drunk!

They were not drunk, they had God's power. Peter went from 3 times denier of Jesus to bold, fearless preacher. It was like the circuit was complete and the switch was flipped.....BOOM!

What about us?

We can follow their example, pray, wait, and we can ask for God's Spirit to fill us. Though we are not perfect, if we seek to be set free from anything that hinders us, clean up our acts and pray together in agreement, then SUDDENLY God's Spirit will move in power.

Individually we need topping up. It's no use constantly running on fumes, doing this in a car ruins the engine. We need to keep a full tank, but we are leaky vessels so there's only one way to do this...stay constantly connected to the Power source, God. Then we can gain strength, have courage, banish fear and begin to work in the ways God wants us to.

So, let's make the connection, join the circuit and flip the switch.

Power up on God's Spirit today!

Based on the Word by Billy Evans 2015

2 BREAD OF HEAVEN

Bread. There are so many different types today. But in Jesus' time it was probably the most important and nutritional source of food.

On Sunday the nation sang **Bread Of Heaven**, to cheer on our rugby team.

We sang it too.

But we also sang it in thanks and praise of the source of all physical, emotional and spiritual nutrition - The Creator of all things, God.

After Jesus had fasted for thirty days, Satan tempted him to turn stones in to bread. He resisted, saying "Man cannot live on bread alone..."

So what else did Jesus say we need to live?

Jesus concluded "....but on every word which comes from the mouth of God"

The disciples were not sure how to pray.

Jesus shared a prayer which is in two main parts. We know it as The Lord's Prayer.

The first is all about acknowledging, praising and thanking The Creator, Father God. The second part deals with our daily needs and struggles; our need to be protected, directed, forgiven and to forgive.

Do you have dogs who are right by your side when you eat, but disappear when it's gone? They just won't come when you call! We shouldn't be like these furry, fair weathered friends!

We should devour the daily bread of God's Word, the Bible, and apply it to all things in life; great and small.

Jesus said we should not worry about food and clothes, but should look for God's direction, and follow it; then all of these things will be provided.

So, rather than missing God's Word, or letting things go stale, we should take time to digest it. Let's not be so distracted by other matters that we fail to spend time reading, praying and listening; which is like skipping meals and allowing birds to swoop in and gobble them up! Let prayer become our regular way, not a knee jerk reaction to trouble.

Let's savor every crumb we receive, relish each moment, and rest in the assurance of God's love. For God will bless us with a feast in the end.

Seek Jesus, The Way, The Truth, The Word and The Life; The True Bread Of Heaven, today!

Based on the Word by Billy Evans 9th February 2016

3 CHANGE

Love it, hate it, dread it, we can't stop it....change.

From the minute we are born we are changing physically. The world around, circumstances, concepts, beliefs, attitudes, constantly changing.

One man was full of hatred.... hatred for the Church, despising Jesus, officiating oppression, setting up stonings, persecuting believers. The least likely man to be a Christian leader was changed after an experience with the one he persecuted.

Physically he was blinded, but spiritually he gained new sight. Saul the oppressor became Paul the faithful follower of Jesus, going literally to great lengths to spread Jesus' message.

We might think we are too far gone, too bad to be changed, too stuck in our ways to detour, too lost, too lonely, too sick. But there is one who can change all things for good, one who themselves are unchangeable.

God is the Lord who does not change. God can change any situation, thing or person.

From hopelessness to hope, from sorrow to joy, from pain to strength.

Never expect two people to be the same. God is at work in us, changing, transforming us into his image. You are unique, you have a purpose, are part of God's plan.

Be patient and optimistic. Don't give up.

We might face fears that are like fires.

Three men were thrown into a furnace because of their faithfulness. Were they abandoned? No!

The King saw another walking in the flames with them, protecting, strengthening, they were unscathed.

The King was changed, praised God, and set a decree that any people, nation or language that spoke against their God shall be cut to pieces! Then the King promoted them. They trusted God; God changed the King's heart.

Having faith isn't easy. It doesn't take life's troubles away, but it gives hope, patience and strength.

We need to be constantly changed. Jesus changes our impurities with his purity.

So, wherever you are today, in the flames of fear, the depths of doubt or depression, struggling with addictions, facing hopelessness, battling bitterness, you do not have to walk alone.

There is one who made you, who loves you, who can walk with you.

Reach out your hand and let your creator in today.

Based on the Word shared by Billy Evans. 31st May 2016

4 BATTLE PRAYER

When circumstances overwhelm you, and life is too much, what do you do?

Jehoshaphat faced a huge army, impossible to defeat. (2 Chronicles 20)

His reaction was to pray, get others in his country to pray, and fast.

He prayed, reminding God of the promises He made.

Imagine if our world leaders did this!

Could we follow Jehoshaphat's example?

When life goes wrong, calamity comes, the world wages war, disease spreads, sickness torments, families face poverty; big or small, remember no problem is too hard to solve with God.

People are powerless in some situations. The only place to look for help is to God, who is all powerful.

In response to Jehoshaphat's prayers: "This is what the Lord says to you: 'Do not be afraid or discouraged because of this vast army. For the battle is not yours, but God's."

When it was time for the battle Jehoshaphat and his people went out singing praise to God, believing the battle could be won by God, despite the odds.

In a twist of events the enemy turned in on themselves, destroying each other!

God can turn problems into blessings, and is a very present help in times of trouble.

God speaks in your acts of faith.

So next time you face fear, think a problem is too big, or a situation too hopeless, cry out for help.

Only God can do the impossible, but we can all do something. Show kindness, encouragement, be there for people, offer what we have.

We might see evil in people, causing hurt in this world, but God is in control; our certain help in times of trouble.

Shout out to God today.

The Word shared by Billy Evans. 26th July 2016

5 STAY CONNECTED

Self-sufficient, independent, isolated, cut off...is this how you live?

Jesus speaks of himself, and us, like a grape vine. He is the vine; we are the branches. Jesus is our source of strength and provision, if we stay connected.

If we cut ourselves off from the source we dry up and soon become useless, fruitless twigs!

What cuts us off? Busyness, bitterness, distractions, disappointments, bad choices....

To keep the vine healthy, and productive, God cuts off the fruitless bits in our lives so, the rest can thrive.

When we feel hurt or sick it can be difficult to focus, to stay connected, but unless we do how will we get the strength to carry on?

Jesus wants us to do more than simply survive, he wants us to live life to the full. And there are two main things we are required to do, to love God and love our neighbours, as we love ourselves.

If we stay connected, spend time with Jesus, the "fruit" of God's Spirit can grow in our lives: Love, joy, peace, patience, kindness, goodness, gentleness and self-control.

But it's not just about us growing and developing, the vine image shows us that God is our provider. As we stay connected to the vine we get just what we need, whatever we ask for, God provides. These are promises from God that we can depend on.

So next time we are struggling or try to go it alone, remember, there's a vine with our name on it, waiting for us to connect!

The Word shared by Billy Evans. 6th December 2016

6 LOVE

What kind of love does God want? How should we live?

Self-centered, empire building, wealth accumulating, uncompassionate lives?

No!

God wants us to love Him and our neighbours.

Jesus was concerned for the poor, those marginalised by society, the outcasts of his day.

His message was to look after the weak, the vulnerable, widows and orphans.

Jesus preached Good News to the poor, not just those poor in wealth but those poor in Spirit... people who feel empty, lost and broken...those hungry to hear.

Jesus wants to give us beauty for the ashes of our lost hope; to restore our broken dreams and heal our hurting hearts. To forgive us for our mistakes.

Do we recognise our needs or are we too busy judging others?

One "religious" man boasted of his exemplary life, he belittled the "sinner" tax collector.

This tax collector poured out his heart to God, he opened himself up – he was honest and humble, recognised he was bankrupt, and needed God.

Are we too busy judging, bearing grudges, thinking of our own achievements that we miss God's message of forgiveness and compassion?

Do we let God do His work in us?

Loving our neighbour, love in general, is costly.

It cost Jesus his life. His sinless soul was stained. His wounds are our healing. His death is our life. His Light dispels our darkness.

If we want love it costs.

There is nothing wrong with being wealthy, unless that wealth rules us…makes us misers, ignoring, judging or despising those who have less.

We may be spiritually bankrupt but full of wealth, or visa versa.

The rich young ruler who spoke to Jesus was too attached to his wealth; he couldn't let it go.

If you are loaded with cash or flat broke, look to what God wants you to do. Share what you have and pray for what you need.

Love others, forgive – turn from what is not good. Follow the right path and do not let anything get in your way.

Be ambassadors for God, whether you are rich or poor.

Show compassion, give hope, let your actions and life choices be fair and just for all people – even if society says you shouldn't.

Above all, Love….

Because Love conquers all!

The Word By Billy Evans 14th February 2017

7 TREE OF LIFE

A beautiful mountain stream, surrounded by glorious countryside. An amazing sight.

A fallen tree in the distance, lying across the stream, appears to blot the landscape, but what if we saw it differently?

What if this calamity offered new hope, a way for us to cross the stream, sending us in a different direction?

Without the fallen tree, there may never have been a way.

In life we hit road blocks, we suffer loss, ill health, disappointments. We make mistakes.

Change isn't always easy.

Trees appear a lot in the Bible. It begins with the Tree of Life and the Tree of Knowledge. Tempted by the devil, the humans disobeyed God's instructions and ate from the forbidden Tree of Knowledge. This had consequences, disobedience put distance between God and mankind.

We live with these consequences as fear, death, hopelessness, "sin" surrounds us.

God didn't end the story here.

There was another tree, one that would reunite us with him and cover our mistakes and bad choices.

That tree is the cross.

Purity personified was crucified on a tree.

Jesus' death brings new life. A way where there was no way. The Way. Our way back to God.

If we accept what Jesus did and ask for forgiveness, we can have a new life of faith and hope.

As we live this new life we still face struggles, pain and hardships. This is where we need to be like the oak tree. Strong, sturdy, secure, with deep roots in God that can withstand any storm.

Trees offer life. They take in CO_2 and give out oxygen that we need to live.

Like trees, we need to take the bad things and wrong choices, and with God's help turn them into something good.

There are many varieties of trees, some good for building, some offer shade, others bear fruit. So it is with us, we are all different but we have a purpose.

Remember, if God has promised something it WILL be done.

Storms are scary, we want to run and hide. Fear is disabling, doubt makes us worry...remember God is working ALL things out for good for those who love Him. God is our strength, our hope, an ever-present presence in times of trouble.

So next time something happens, remember the fallen tree.

Pray for hope and a new way, fulfilling the promises of God.

Draw your strength from Jesus, soak up His light and life today.

The Word shared by Billy 30th May 2017

8 IT IS WELL WITH MY SOUL

Life can be overwhelming. The pain of loss, grief, disappointment, sickness, hurt, we feel we can't go on, but there is hope.

Jesus faced unbearable pain, He knew it was coming, He chose and embraced it....the cross. The cross wasn't just capital punishment, Jesus took mankind's punishment. The agony of a perfect, spotless, soul soiled by the filth of greed, envy, injustice and worse...the punishment for all our faults, laid on Jesus, God as a man on earth, to make a way for us to be free.

When we go through hard times, Jesus knows. Jesus knows your pain; He can heal you. He knows your hurt; He can comfort you. He knows your fear, He can give you peace.

Jesus is The Way.

After the agony Jesus looked up to heaven saying "It is finished". This was not the end but the beginning. A new way for all of us to be connected to God without religious rituals, guilt or fear, just love. A way for our Helper to step in, God's Spirit. We are no longer alone, burdened by our wrongs, trying to earn a way to God. Jesus is that way.

Jesus faced unbearable pain. Eventually it was finished. We face unbearable things. Each day an agony. In the midst of pain, look up. Seek Jesus, the comforter, He'll give you strength. We can do ALL things with His help, nothing is impossible. Darkness covers us for a time but joy comes in the morning.

Apostle Paul said he rejoiced in the Lord in whatever state he was in, he'd learned to be content when he was full or hungry, rich or poor, sick or well.

Horatio Spafford, Chicago, lost his 4 year old son, then in the great fire he lost his thriving business.

His wife went on a boat to England, it sank and their 4 daughters died, his wife survived.

As Spafford travelled to England, he wrote the now famous hymn "*It is well with my soul*".

He didn't go against God, he mourned but didn't give up. Later he had more children and helped to set up various charitable organisations benefiting many.

No matter what's happened in the past, now or in the future, know one thing: Jesus can give you strength to do all things! Take your eyes off circumstances and look to the cross. A time of loss can become a time of hope and peace. It is finished. Good things will begin. Keep your eyes on Jesus, know it is well with your soul today!

The Word shared by Billy Evans in 2017

9 CAST YOU CARES

Are you worn out with worry, straining with stress, feeling you can't go on?

Jesus tells us to cast our worries on Him because He cares for us.

How do we do this?

Casting in sea fishing means throwing out the line as far as possible, letting it go.

We can tell Jesus all that bothers us, hand it all over to him.

We might do this for a bit, but later claw worries back! We dwell on negative thoughts, think the worst, let go of hope and spiral into worry. It's a battle. We must combat negative thoughts with God's promises: I will provide, I am with you, you can do all things through Christ who strengthens you....

When we are weary, getting depressed, we need to come to Jesus and get back into his agenda, purposes and plans.

Plans God has for us are good, so trust. Sometimes good things we want might not be in God's agenda. It has to be not your will, but Gods.

Psalm 37 says Rest in the Lord, don't fret; trust and wait for God to sort things out.

Isaiah 40 promises that God gives power to the weak, so we can soar above storms like eagles do, as God renews our strength. This only happens as we trust God.

In a world of instant coffee, we want things now! We wonder why things are slow. We have to submit, hand it all over.

We were created in Jesus to do the good works prepared for us.

Before a vision of God's plans becomes clear God will give you a glimpse, like a picture developing. Keep moving forward, stay in communication with God. Pray for glimpses of the future, patience, and faith to trust that

God is working for your good.

Getting weary comes to us all. Jesus says go to Him with wrongs, worries, weariness and somehow, someday, everything changes. Jesus takes on our problems, carries our concerns, has paid for our mistakes in full, no need for guilt!

Suffering in prison, Paul reminded the Philippians to rejoice in the Lord always; don't moan, that'll set us back!

We can't always see everything, things look bleak. We need blind faith, trust that God is good and wants the best for us who love him.

Pray, request, cry out, shout! Cast those worries, don't take them back, and God's peace that surpasses understanding will be with you today.

The Word shared by Billy Evans 10th October 2017

10 EARTHQUAKES

When earthquakes hit, they might just shake us up a bit; sometimes their affects can be devastating.

Sometimes life shakes us up, disturbs our peace, makes us anxious and afraid: bad news, illness, pain, suffering loss or hurt. Perhaps, like the earthquake, there's something at fault with us.

We can find rest in the fact that God loves us.

In the upper room John sat, resting his head on Jesus, what a place to be. After Jesus' crucifixion it's reported they hid in a room in fear. Jesus came and stood in their midst, He didn't tell them off, He said: "Peace be with you."

If we haven't got peace, we've got nothing.

If we have peace, we have it all. Jesus gives His peace, in spite of challenges.

Faith is the foundation of everything. If we lay foundations to build a house and have all the materials around, but don't build up, it's a waste. We should always be building ourselves and each-other up.

"But you, dear friends, carefully build yourselves up in this most holy faith by praying in the Holy Spirit, staying right at the center of God's love, keeping your arms open and outstretched, ready for the mercy of our Master, Jesus Christ. This is the unending life, the real life!" Jude 1: 20-21.

If you feel flat it's time to build yourselves up! Pray, have faith and trust God. We can pray for strength and wisdom. We might pray in private, calling out to God from our heart, with the help of the Holy Spirit; or pray for others, with other believers, or ask for prayer for ourselves.

Remember: God loves us, we should love one-another as He loves us. We are not servants but friends, chosen by God to bear fruit. Give things over to God, if you have a need, ask. Be faithful and whatever you ask God, it will be given.

Stay connected, pray in all circumstances, study God's Word, meditate on God's promises.

Faith leads on to other things. Without action, faith is worthless.

On Earth the building never ends, in heaven everything is ready.

A measure of faith is given to all, but don't just settle for a measure, desire more from God.

Start building on your faith today.

The Word by Billy Evans 19th February 2018

ABOUT THE AUTHOR
William (Billy) Evans

William (Billy) Evans was a Welsh Christian man who loved God's Word, the Bible. During his life, on many occasions, Billy shared his reflections on The Word of God.

This book shares some of Billy Evans' reflections on God's Word. Each piece was recorded and written by Sharron Hardwick, when Billy Evans shared them as part of the New Life Christian Fellowship Pembrokeshire meetings.

In good times and bad Billy's reflections of The Word remind us that God never leaves us, He can carry us through the storms of life, feed us with daily bread, and bring us joy and peace in all circumstances.

A man of strong faith in Jesus, Billy, like God's Word, now lives forever, in the hearts of his loved ones and in the arms of his saviour.

ABOUT THE AUTHOR
Sharron Hardwick

Sharron Hardwick is a writer and author.

Sharron writes Church, charity, sports reports and Fairtrade articles for local press. She is the Founder of the *Fair Trade In Football Campaign www.fairtradeinfootball.com* and is the author of *"Gideon The Super Cat - The Quest For Truth"*.

Sharron wrote these reflections on God's Word, which were shared by Billy Evans as part of the New Life Christian Fellowship Pembrokeshire meetings. These *Gleanings* were printed in the *Tenby Observer,* shared on *New Life Church Facebook Group* and line at *newlifechurchpembs.com*

"In loving memory of our dear friend Billy.

May these words live forever, giving light, encouragement and hope.

May they bless you and give you new life as they reflect Jesus and His everlasting love."

Sharron Hardwick

"So shall my word be that goes out from my mouth;
it shall not return to me empty,
but it shall accomplish that which I purpose,
and shall succeed in the thing for which I sent it." Isaiah 55:11

Printed in Great Britain
by Amazon